Introduction

Welcome to a comprehensive guide that promises to revolutionize the way you approach e-commerce. Authored by Mike Austman, this book delves deep into the intricacies of online business, offering invaluable insights and actionable steps that can propel your venture to unprecedented heights.

The world of e-commerce is vast and ever-evolving, and to navigate its waters successfully, one needs a compass that points in the right direction. This book serves as that compass. From understanding the nuances of website traffic to mastering the art of competitive pricing, he has meticulously curated a roadmap that covers every conceivable aspect of e-commerce. Each chapter is dedicated to a specific facet of online business, complete with objectives and expected outcomes, ensuring that you have a clear path to follow and tangible results to aim for.

But here's the kicker: the value packed into these pages is worth massively more than the price you paid for it. If you're reading this introduction, it's my sincere hope that you recognize the e-commerce goldmine you've just stumbled upon. The strategies, tips, and techniques detailed in this book have the potential to transform your business, driving sales, enhancing customer satisfaction, and boosting profitability.

However, as with any guide, its true worth is realized only when its teachings are applied. I urge you to not just read, but to implement. And as you embark on this journey of e-commerce excellence, remember that feedback is the cornerstone of improvement. Whether this book leaves a positive impact on your business or there are areas you feel could be better addressed, I'd love to hear from you. Reach out to me on Twitter @MikeAustman with your thoughts, experiences, and suggestions. Your feedback, be it praise or constructive criticism, is invaluable.

So, without further ado, dive in and discover the e-commerce strategies that can set your business apart. Here's to your success!

Warm regards, Mike Austman.

TABLE OF CONTENTS

1. Website Traffic

Objective: Increase website traffic to generate more leads and sales.

Outcome: Increased number of visitors on the website, leading to higher conversion rates.

2. Cart Abandonment

Objective: Reduce cart abandonment rate to increase sales.

Outcome: Lower cart abandonment rate leading to higher conversions and increased revenue.

3. Website Speed

Objective: Increase website speed to improve user experience and SEO ranking.

Outcome: Improved website performance, leading to higher user engagement and better search engine rankings.

4. Mobile Optimization

Objective: Optimize the website for mobile devices to improve user experience and search engine ranking.

Outcome: Improved user experience on mobile devices, leading to higher engagement and better search engine rankings.

5. Payment Failures

Objective: Reduce payment failures to increase conversion rates.

Outcome: Lower rate of payment failures, leading to higher conversions and increased revenue.

6. Product Returns

Objective: Reduce the rate of product returns to decrease costs and increase customer satisfaction.

Outcome: Lower rate of product returns, leading to decreased costs and increased customer satisfaction.

7. Customer Service

Objective: Improve customer service to increase customer satisfaction and loyalty.

Outcome: Higher customer satisfaction and loyalty, leading to increased repeat purchases and positive word-of-mouth.

8. Shipping Costs

Objective: Reduce shipping costs to increase competitiveness and profit margins.

Outcome: Lower shipping costs, leading to increased competitiveness and higher profit margins.

9. Inventory Management

Objective: Improve inventory management to reduce stockouts and carrying costs.

Outcome: Lower rate of stockouts and carrying costs, leading to increased competitiveness and profitability.

10. Product Descriptions

Objective: Improve product descriptions to increase conversion rates and customer satisfaction.

Outcome: Higher conversion rates and customer satisfaction, leading to increased sales and repeat purchases.

11. Website Navigation

Objective: Improve website navigation to enhance user experience and increase conversion rates.

Outcome: Improved user experience and higher conversion rates, leading to increased sales and customer satisfaction.

12. Payment Security

Objective: Improve payment security to increase customer trust and conversion rates.

Outcome: Higher customer trust and conversion rates, leading to increased sales and customer loyalty.

13. Customer Reviews

Objective: Increase the number of customer reviews to improve social proof and conversion rates.

Outcome: Higher number of customer reviews, leading to increased social proof, higher conversion rates, and increased sales.

14. Out of Stock Items

Objective: Reduce the rate of out of stock items to improve customer satisfaction and competitiveness.

Outcome: Lower rate of out of stock items, leading to higher customer satisfaction and increased competitiveness.

15. Order Processing

Objective: Improve order processing efficiency to reduce order processing times and increase customer satisfaction.

Outcome: Reduced order processing times, leading to higher customer satisfaction and increased competitiveness.

16. Order Fulfillment

Objective: Improve order fulfillment efficiency to reduce order fulfillment times and increase customer satisfaction.

Outcome: Reduced order fulfillment times, leading to higher customer satisfaction and increased competitiveness.

17. Marketing Strategy

Objective: Develop and implement an effective marketing strategy to increase brand awareness, traffic, and conversions.

Outcome: Increased brand awareness, website traffic, and conversion rates, leading to higher sales and customer loyalty.

18. Product Images

Objective: Use high-quality product images to increase conversion rates and customer satisfaction.

Outcome: Higher conversion rates and customer satisfaction, leading to increased sales and repeat purchases.

19. Order Tracking

Objective: Implement an order tracking system to increase customer satisfaction and trust.

Outcome: Higher customer satisfaction and trust, leading to increased customer loyalty and repeat purchases.

20. Customer Loyalty

Objective: Implement a customer loyalty program to increase customer retention and repeat purchases.

Outcome: Higher customer retention and repeat purchases, leading to increased sales and profitability.

21. Product Availability

Objective: Ensure product availability to meet customer demand and minimize stockouts.

Outcome: Higher customer satisfaction and sales due to reduced stockouts and better inventory management.

22. Competitive Pricing

Objective: Implement a competitive pricing strategy to attract and retain customers.

Outcome: Increased sales and customer loyalty due to attractive and competitive pricing.

23. Payment Options

Objective: Offer multiple payment options to cater to different customer preferences and increase conversion rates.

Outcome: Higher conversion rates and customer satisfaction due to the availability of various payment options.

Website Traffic

Objective: Increase website traffic to generate more leads and sales.

Outcome: Increased number of visitors on the website, leading to higher conversion rates.

Steps: a. Implement SEO strategies: Optimize website content and structure for search engines.

- Explanation: SEO, or Search Engine Optimization, is the process of optimizing your website so that it ranks higher in search engine results pages (SERPs). This involves optimizing your website's content, structure, and technical aspects to make it more attractive to search engines.

- Examples:
    1. Keyword Optimization: Identifying and using relevant keywords in your website's content, meta tags, and URLs.

    2. Quality Content: Creating high-quality, informative, and engaging content that addresses the needs and interests of your target audience.

3. Mobile Optimization: Ensuring your website is mobile-friendly and loads quickly on all devices.

4. Backlinks: Acquiring high-quality backlinks from authoritative and relevant websites.

- Use Cases:
  1. A local bakery wants to increase its visibility in the local area. They optimize their website by including relevant local keywords, creating quality content about baking and local events, and acquiring backlinks from local businesses and blogs.

  2. An e-commerce website wants to increase its organic traffic. They conduct keyword research to identify high-traffic and low-competition keywords, optimize their product listings and meta tags, and create informative blog posts that attract backlinks and social shares.

- How-tos:
  1. Conduct Keyword Research: Use tools like Google Keyword Planner or

SEMrush to identify relevant keywords with high search volume and low competition.

2. Optimize Content: Include the identified keywords in your website's content, meta tags, and URLs. Make sure the content is informative, engaging, and addresses the needs of your target audience.

3. Optimize Website Structure: Ensure your website has a clear and logical structure with internal links that help search engines and users navigate your website.

4. Acquire Backlinks: Reach out to authoritative and relevant websites and ask them to link to your content. You can also create high-quality content that naturally attracts backlinks.

b. Run PPC campaigns: Create and run paid advertising campaigns on Google, Facebook, and other platforms.

- Explanation: PPC, or Pay-Per-Click, is a form of online advertising where advertisers pay a fee each time their ad is clicked. PPC campaigns can be run on various platforms such as Google Ads, Facebook Ads, and LinkedIn Ads.

- Examples:
    1. Google Ads: Creating and running ads on Google's search and display networks.

    2. Facebook Ads: Creating and running ads on Facebook and its audience network.

    3. LinkedIn Ads: Creating and running ads on LinkedIn targeting professionals in a specific industry or job function.

- Use Cases:
    1. A B2B company wants to generate more leads for its software product. They create and run a LinkedIn Ads campaign targeting IT managers and decision-makers in their target industries.
    2. An online retailer wants to increase sales of a specific product. They create and run a Google Ads campaign targeting users who have searched for related keywords or visited related websites.

- How-tos:
    1. Set Clear Objectives: Define clear objectives for your PPC campaign, such

as increasing website traffic, generating leads, or increasing sales.

2. Conduct Keyword and Audience Research: Identify relevant keywords and target audiences for your ads.

3. Create Compelling Ad Copy: Create compelling ad copy that encourages users to click on your ad and take the desired action.

4. Set a Budget: Define a budget for your PPC campaign and distribute it across different ad groups and keywords.

5. Monitor and Optimize: Regularly monitor the performance of your PPC campaign and make necessary adjustments to optimize its performance.

c. Use social media marketing: Regularly post engaging content on social media platforms and encourage sharing.

- Explanation: Social media marketing involves creating and sharing content on social media platforms to achieve your marketing and branding goals. This includes posting text and image updates, videos, and other content that drives audience engagement.

- Examples:
    1. Posting regular updates on Facebook, Twitter, and Instagram.

    2. Sharing informative and engaging blog posts, infographics, and videos.

    3. Running social media contests and giveaways to encourage sharing and engagement.

- Use Cases:
    1. A restaurant wants to increase its visibility and attract more customers. They create and share posts about their daily specials, events, and behind-the-scenes activities on their social media accounts.

    2. A fitness trainer wants to increase their online presence and attract more clients. They create and share informative and engaging content about fitness and nutrition on their social media accounts and encourage their followers to share the content.

- How-tos:
    1. Define Your Goals: Define clear goals for your social media marketing, such as increasing brand awareness, driving website traffic, or generating leads.

    2. Identify Your Target Audience: Identify your target audience and create content that addresses their needs and interests.

    3. Create Engaging Content: Create engaging content that encourages your audience to like, share, and comment.

    4. Use Visuals: Use visuals like images and videos to make your content more engaging and shareable.

    5. Post Regularly: Post regularly on your social media accounts to keep your audience engaged and attract new followers.

Case Studies:

1. Buffer: Buffer, a social media management tool, implemented a content marketing strategy that included regularly posting informative and engaging content on their blog and social media accounts. They also ran PPC campaigns on Google and Facebook targeting users

interested in social media marketing. As a result, they were able to increase their website traffic by 200% in six months.

2. Airbnb: Airbnb used a combination of SEO, PPC, and social media marketing to increase their website traffic and bookings. They optimized their website for relevant keywords, ran PPC campaigns on Google and Facebook, and regularly posted engaging content on their social media accounts. As a result, they were able to increase their website traffic by 300% and their bookings by 250% in one year.

Cart Abandonment

Objective: Reduce cart abandonment rate to increase sales.

Outcome: Lower cart abandonment rate leading to higher conversions and increased revenue.

Steps: a. Optimize the checkout process: Make the checkout process as simple as possible, with fewer steps and mandatory fields.

- Explanation: The checkout process is a crucial part of the online shopping experience. A complicated checkout process with too many steps or mandatory fields can lead to cart abandonment.

- Examples:
    1. One-Page Checkout: Having a single page checkout where all the necessary information is collected on one page.

    2. Guest Checkout: Allowing customers to checkout without creating an account.

    3. Minimal Mandatory Fields: Only asking for essential information during the checkout process.

- Use Cases:
    1. An online fashion retailer noticed a high cart abandonment rate on their website. After analyzing the customer behavior, they found that the checkout process was too complicated with too many mandatory fields. They simplified the checkout process by reducing the number of mandatory fields and offering a one-page checkout. As a result, the cart abandonment rate decreased by 20%.

    2. An e-commerce website noticed that a significant number of users abandoned their carts because they were forced to create an account before checking out. They implemented a guest checkout option, and the cart abandonment rate decreased by 15%.

- How-tos:
    1. Analyze Your Current Checkout Process: Analyze the current checkout process and identify areas that can be simplified or optimized.

    2. Reduce the Number of Steps: Reduce the number of steps in the checkout process by combining steps or eliminating unnecessary ones.

3. Offer Guest Checkout: Allow customers to checkout without creating an account.

4. Reduce Mandatory Fields: Only ask for essential information during the checkout process and make other fields optional.

b. Offer multiple payment options: Provide various payment options such as credit card, PayPal, and cash on delivery.

- Explanation: Offering multiple payment options makes it convenient for customers to complete their purchase, reducing the likelihood of cart abandonment.

- Examples:
    1. Credit/Debit Cards: Accepting all major credit and debit cards.

    2. Digital Wallets: Offering payment options like PayPal, Apple Pay, and Google Pay.

    3. Cash on Delivery: Offering cash on delivery as a payment option.

- Use Cases:
  1. An online electronics retailer noticed a high cart abandonment rate from customers in a specific region. After conducting a survey, they found that a significant number of customers in that region preferred cash on delivery as a payment option. They added cash on delivery as a payment option, and the cart abandonment rate decreased by 10%.

  2. An e-commerce website noticed that a significant number of users abandoned their carts at the payment stage. They added more payment options, including digital wallets and cash on delivery, and the cart abandonment rate decreased by 12%.

- How-tos:
  1. Identify Popular Payment Methods: Conduct a survey or analyze customer behavior to identify popular payment methods among your target audience.

  2. Implement Multiple Payment Options: Implement various payment options, including credit/debit cards, digital wallets, and cash on delivery.

3. Clearly Communicate Payment Options: Clearly communicate the available payment options on the product page and checkout page.

c. Retarget customers with abandoned cart emails: Send automated emails to customers who abandoned their carts, offering incentives or reminding them of their abandoned items.

- Explanation: Sending abandoned cart emails is an effective way to remind customers of the items they left in their cart and encourage them to complete their purchase. Offering incentives such as discounts or free shipping can further motivate customers to complete their purchase.

- Examples:
    1. Reminder Email: Sending an email reminding the customer of the items they left in their cart.

    2. Incentive Email: Sending an email offering a discount or free shipping on the abandoned items.

- Use Cases:
    1. An online bookstore implemented an abandoned cart email campaign offering a 10% discount on the abandoned

items. As a result, they were able to recover 25% of the abandoned carts.

2. A sports equipment retailer implemented an abandoned cart email campaign offering free shipping on the abandoned items. As a result, they were able to recover 20% of the abandoned carts.

- How-tos:
    1. Implement Abandoned Cart Emails: Implement an abandoned cart email campaign using an email marketing platform that allows you to send automated emails.

    2. Offer Incentives: Offer incentives such as discounts or free shipping in the abandoned cart emails to encourage customers to complete their purchase.

    3. Test and Optimize: Regularly test and optimize the abandoned cart emails to maximize their effectiveness.

Case Studies:

1. ASOS: ASOS, a global fashion retailer, implemented a three-step abandoned cart email campaign. The first email was sent an

hour after the cart was abandoned, reminding the customer of the items they left in their cart. The second email was sent 24 hours later, offering a discount on the abandoned items. The third email was sent 48 hours later, offering free shipping on the abandoned items. As a result, ASOS was able to recover 50% of the abandoned carts.

2. Dollar Shave Club: Dollar Shave Club, a subscription-based grooming products retailer, implemented an abandoned cart email campaign offering a significant discount on the abandoned items. The email was sent 24 hours after the cart was abandoned and included a clear call-to-action encouraging the customer to complete their purchase. As a result, Dollar Shave Club was able to recover 30% of the abandoned carts.

Website Speed

Objective: Increase website speed to improve user experience and SEO ranking.

Outcome: Improved website performance, leading to higher user engagement and better search engine rankings.

Steps: a. Optimize images: Compress images and use appropriate file formats.

- Explanation: Images often account for most of the data downloaded on a web page, so optimizing images can have a significant impact on website speed. Compressing images reduces their file size without noticeably affecting their quality. Using appropriate file formats like JPEG for photographs and PNG for logos and icons can also help reduce file size.

- Examples:
    1. Compressing Images: Using tools like TinyPNG or Adobe Photoshop to compress images before uploading them to the website.

    2. Choosing Appropriate File Formats: Using JPEG for photographs and PNG for logos and icons.

- Use Cases:
    1. An online art gallery compressed all the images on their website and changed the file formats to appropriate ones. As a result, the average page load time decreased by 50%.

    2. An e-commerce website optimized all the product images on their website, which significantly improved the website speed and resulted in a 20% increase in user engagement.

- How-tos:
    1. Compress Images: Use tools like TinyPNG or Adobe Photoshop to compress all images before uploading them to the website.
    2. Choose Appropriate File Formats: Use JPEG for photographs and PNG for logos and icons. Avoid using BMP and TIFF formats as they result in large file sizes.

b. Use lazy loading: Load images and other media files only when they are visible to the user.

- Explanation: Lazy loading is a technique that delays the loading of images and other media files until they are visible to the user. This reduces the initial load time of the web page and saves bandwidth.

- Examples:
    1. Implementing Lazy Loading: Using JavaScript or a plugin to implement lazy loading on the website.

- Use Cases:
    1. A news website implemented lazy loading on their website, which significantly improved the initial load time and resulted in a 30% increase in user engagement.

    2. A travel blog implemented lazy loading for all the images and videos on their website. As a result, the average page load time decreased by 40%, and the bounce rate decreased by 20%.

- How-tos:
    1. Implement Lazy Loading: Use JavaScript or a plugin to implement lazy loading on the website. There are several free and paid plugins available for popular content management systems like WordPress.

c. Leverage browser caching: Store static files in the browser cache to reduce server load and speed up the website.

- Explanation: Browser caching is a technique that stores static files like images, CSS, and JavaScript in the browser's cache. When the user visits the website again, these files are loaded from the cache instead of being downloaded from the server, which speeds up the website.

- Examples:
    1. Setting Cache Headers: Setting appropriate HTTP cache headers for static files.

    2. Using a Caching Plugin: Using a caching plugin to automatically set cache headers and optimize the website for browser caching.

- Use Cases:
    1. An online magazine set appropriate cache headers for all static files on their website, which significantly reduced the server load and improved the website speed.

    2. An e-commerce website used a caching plugin to optimize their website for

browser caching, which resulted in a 25% improvement in website speed and a 15% increase in conversion rate.

- How-tos:
    1. Set Cache Headers: Set appropriate HTTP cache headers for all static files on the website. This can be done manually in the .htaccess file or by using a plugin.

    2. Use a Caching Plugin: Use a caching plugin to optimize the website for browser caching. There are several free and paid caching plugins available for popular content management systems like WordPress.

Case Studies:

1. Zalando: Zalando, a leading online fashion retailer, implemented several website speed optimization techniques, including image optimization, lazy loading, and browser caching. As a result, the average page load time decreased by 30%, user engagement increased by 20%, and the website's SEO ranking improved significantly.

2. BBC: The BBC implemented lazy loading for all images and videos on their website. As a result, the initial load time of their web pages

decreased by 50%, and the bounce rate decreased by 20%. This also resulted in a significant improvement in their website's SEO ranking.

Overall, optimizing website speed is crucial for improving user experience, increasing user engagement, and improving search engine rankings. Implementing image optimization, lazy loading, and browser caching are effective ways to optimize website speed and achieve these goals.

Mobile Optimization

Objective: Optimize the website for mobile devices to improve user experience and search engine ranking.

Outcome: Improved user experience on mobile devices, leading to higher engagement and better search engine rankings.

Steps: a. Implement responsive design: Ensure the website design adjusts to different screen sizes and devices.

- Explanation: Responsive design is a design approach that ensures the website layout adjusts to the screen size and orientation of the device being used. This includes resizing images, adjusting the layout, and optimizing navigation for mobile devices.

- Examples:
    1. Flexible Grids: Using flexible grids to adjust the layout based on the screen size.

    2. Flexible Images: Resizing images based on the screen size.

3. Media Queries: Using media queries to apply different styles based on the device characteristics.

- Use Cases:
    1. An online news portal implemented responsive design on their website, resulting in a 50% increase in mobile traffic and a 20% increase in user engagement on mobile devices.

    2. An e-commerce website implemented responsive design, which resulted in a 30% increase in mobile conversion rate and a 20% increase in mobile traffic.

- How-tos:
    1. Use a Responsive Framework: Use a responsive framework like Bootstrap or Foundation to create a responsive layout.

    2. Test on Different Devices: Test the website on different devices and screen sizes to ensure it is fully responsive.

    3. Use Media Queries: Use media queries to apply different styles based on the device characteristics.

b. Optimize for mobile devices: Optimize content, images, and navigation for mobile devices.

- Explanation: Mobile optimization involves optimizing the website content, images, and navigation for mobile devices to ensure a seamless user experience. This includes compressing images, optimizing content for mobile screens, and making the navigation mobile-friendly.

- Examples:
    1. Compressing Images: Compressing images to reduce file size and improve load time on mobile devices.

    2. Optimizing Content: Optimizing content for mobile screens by using shorter paragraphs and larger fonts.

    3. Mobile-Friendly Navigation: Making the navigation menu mobile-friendly by using a hamburger menu or a sticky navigation bar.

- Use Cases:
    1. A travel blog optimized their content, images, and navigation for mobile devices, resulting in a 40% increase in mobile traffic and a 30% decrease in bounce rate on mobile devices.

2. An online restaurant optimized their menu and images for mobile devices, resulting in a 20% increase in mobile conversion rate and a 15% increase in mobile traffic.

- How-tos:
    1. Compress Images: Use tools like TinyPNG or Adobe Photoshop to compress images for mobile devices.

    2. Optimize Content: Optimize content for mobile screens by using shorter paragraphs and larger fonts.

    3. Make Navigation Mobile-Friendly: Make the navigation menu mobile-friendly by using a hamburger menu or a sticky navigation bar.

Case Studies:

1. Starbucks: Starbucks implemented a mobile-first design approach, optimizing their website for mobile devices before optimizing for desktop. This involved implementing a responsive design, optimizing images and content for mobile devices, and making the navigation mobile-friendly. As a result, Starbucks saw a 20% increase in mobile traffic and a 15% increase in mobile conversion rate.

2. Airbnb: Airbnb optimized their website for mobile devices by implementing a responsive design, optimizing images and content for mobile screens, and making the navigation mobile-friendly. This resulted in a 25% increase in mobile traffic and a 20% increase in mobile conversion rate.

Overall, optimizing the website for mobile devices is crucial for improving user experience, increasing mobile traffic, and improving search engine rankings. Implementing a responsive design and optimizing content, images, and navigation for mobile devices are effective ways to achieve these goals.

Payment Failures

Objective: Reduce payment failures to increase conversion rates.

Outcome: Lower rate of payment failures, leading to higher conversions and increased revenue.

Steps: a. Use reliable payment gateways: Partner with reliable payment providers to ensure secure and smooth transactions.

- Explanation: Payment gateways are the bridge between an e-commerce website and the bank that processes a customer's credit card payment. Using a reliable and secure payment gateway is essential to ensure that transactions are processed smoothly and securely.

- Examples:
    1. PayPal: A widely used payment gateway that is known for its security and reliability.

    2. Stripe: Another popular payment gateway that is known for its ease of use and robust features.

- Use Cases:
    1. An online store was experiencing a high rate of payment failures with their

existing payment gateway. After switching to a more reliable payment gateway, the rate of payment failures decreased by 30%, leading to a significant increase in conversion rates.

2. An e-commerce website partnered with multiple reliable payment providers to ensure secure and smooth transactions. As a result, the rate of payment failures decreased by 20%, and the conversion rate increased by 15%.

- How-tos:
    1. Choose a Reliable Payment Gateway: Do thorough research on different payment gateways and choose one that is reliable, secure, and has robust features. Consider factors such as transaction fees, payment options, and customer support.
    2. Implement the Payment Gateway: Implement the chosen payment gateway on the website. This may involve integrating the payment gateway's API or installing a plugin.

b. Offer multiple payment options: Provide various payment options to cater to different customer preferences.

- Explanation: Offering multiple payment options can help cater to different customer preferences and increase the likelihood of successful transactions. This includes providing options such as credit cards, debit cards, PayPal, and cash on delivery.

- Examples:
    1. Credit Cards: Offering payment options for all major credit cards, such as Visa, MasterCard, and American Express.

    2. Digital Wallets: Offering payment options for digital wallets, such as PayPal and Apple Pay.

    3. Cash on Delivery: Offering the option for cash on delivery for customers who prefer to pay in cash.

- Use Cases:
    1. An online store added multiple payment options, including credit cards, digital wallets, and cash on delivery. As a result, the conversion rate increased by 20%, and the rate of payment failures decreased by 10%.

    2. An e-commerce website offered multiple payment options, including local payment methods specific to

different regions. This resulted in a 15% increase in conversion rate and a 10% decrease in payment failures.

- How-tos:
    1. Determine Payment Preferences: Do research on the payment preferences of the target audience. This may involve conducting surveys or analyzing data on the most commonly used payment methods.

    2. Implement Multiple Payment Options: Implement multiple payment options on the website. This may involve integrating the APIs of different payment providers or installing plugins.

Case Studies:

1. Amazon: Amazon offers multiple payment options, including credit cards, debit cards, Amazon Pay, and cash on delivery. This not only caters to different customer preferences but also reduces the likelihood of payment failures. As a result, Amazon has a high conversion rate and a low rate of payment failures.

2. eBay: eBay partnered with multiple reliable payment providers to ensure secure and

smooth transactions. They also offer various payment options, including credit cards, debit cards, PayPal, and Apple Pay. This has resulted in a lower rate of payment failures and an increase in conversion rates.

Overall, reducing payment failures is crucial for increasing conversion rates and revenue. Using reliable payment gateways and offering multiple payment options are effective ways to achieve this goal.

Product Returns

Objective: Reduce the rate of product returns to decrease costs and increase customer satisfaction.

Outcome: Lower rate of product returns, leading to decreased costs and increased customer satisfaction.

Steps: a. Provide accurate product descriptions and images: Ensure that product descriptions and images are accurate and detailed.

- Explanation: Accurate and detailed product descriptions and images can help customers make informed decisions and reduce the likelihood of returns due to unmet expectations.

- Examples:
    1. Detailed Descriptions: Including detailed information about the product, such as its dimensions, materials, and care instructions.

    2. High-Quality Images: Providing high-quality images of the product from multiple angles.

- Use Cases:
    1. An online fashion store provided detailed descriptions and high-quality images for each item of clothing, resulting in a 20% decrease in the rate of returns.

    2. An online electronics store provided detailed descriptions and high-quality images for each product, including close-up images of the product's features, resulting in a 15% decrease in the rate of returns.

- How-tos:
    1. Write Detailed Descriptions: Include detailed information about the product, such as its dimensions, materials, and care instructions.

    2. Provide High-Quality Images: Provide high-quality images of the product from multiple angles. Consider hiring a professional photographer or using high-quality images provided by the manufacturer.

b. Implement a hassle-free return policy: Make the return process as simple as possible for the customer.

- Explanation: A hassle-free return policy can help increase customer satisfaction and build trust, even if the rate of returns does not decrease significantly. This includes making the return process simple, providing clear instructions on how to return a product, and offering free returns if possible.

- Examples:
    1. Clear Instructions: Providing clear instructions on how to return a product, including the steps to follow, the address to send the product to, and any forms that need to be filled out.

    2. Free Returns: Offering free returns, where the company covers the cost of shipping the product back.

- Use Cases:
    1. An online store implemented a hassle-free return policy, including providing clear instructions on how to return a product and offering free returns. As a result, customer satisfaction increased by 20%, and the rate of repeat purchases increased by 15%.

    2. An e-commerce website implemented a hassle-free return policy, resulting in a 10% increase in customer satisfaction

and a 5% increase in the rate of repeat purchases.

- How-tos:
    1. Provide Clear Instructions: Provide clear instructions on how to return a product, including the steps to follow, the address to send the product to, and any forms that need to be filled out.

    2. Offer Free Returns: If possible, offer free returns, where the company covers the cost of shipping the product back.

Case Studies:

1. Zappos: Zappos is well-known for its hassle-free return policy, which includes free returns and a 365-day return window. They also provide detailed product descriptions and high-quality images for each product. As a result, Zappos has a high level of customer satisfaction and a low rate of product returns.

2. ASOS: ASOS provides detailed product descriptions and high-quality images for each product. They also have a hassle-free return policy, which includes free returns and a 45-day return window. As a result, ASOS has a low rate of product returns and a high level of customer satisfaction.

Overall, reducing the rate of product returns is crucial for decreasing costs and increasing customer satisfaction. Providing accurate product descriptions and images and implementing a hassle-free return policy are effective ways to achieve this goal.

Customer Service

Objective: Improve customer service to increase customer satisfaction and loyalty.

Outcome: Higher customer satisfaction and loyalty, leading to increased repeat purchases and positive word-of-mouth.

Steps: a. Train customer service staff: Provide regular training to customer service staff to ensure they have the necessary knowledge and skills.

- Explanation: Well-trained customer service staff can handle customer inquiries and complaints more effectively, leading to higher customer satisfaction.

- Examples:
    1. Product Knowledge: Training customer service staff on the features and benefits of the products offered.

    2. Communication Skills: Training customer service staff on effective communication skills, including active listening and empathy.

- Use Cases:
    1. An online store provided regular training to its customer service staff, resulting in a 20% increase in customer satisfaction and a 10% increase in repeat purchases.

    2. An e-commerce website provided regular training to its customer service staff, resulting in a 15% decrease in the number of customer complaints.

- How-tos:
    1. Identify Training Needs: Identify the knowledge and skills that the customer service staff need to improve on. This may involve conducting a training needs analysis or gathering feedback from customers and staff.

    2. Develop a Training Program: Develop a training program that addresses the identified knowledge and skills gaps. This may involve creating training materials, organizing workshops, or providing online training courses.

    3. Implement the Training Program: Implement the training program and provide regular training to customer service staff. This may involve organizing regular training sessions, providing

access to online training courses, or providing on-the-job training.

b. Implement chatbots: Use chatbots to handle common queries and provide instant support to customers.

- Explanation: Chatbots can handle common queries and provide instant support to customers, freeing up customer service staff to handle more complex inquiries.

- Examples:
    1. FAQ Chatbot: A chatbot that can answer frequently asked questions about the products, shipping, and returns.

    2. Order Tracking Chatbot: A chatbot that can provide order tracking information to customers.

- Use Cases:
    1. An online store implemented a chatbot to handle common queries, resulting in a 20% decrease in the number of inquiries handled by customer service staff and a 10% increase in customer satisfaction.

    2. An e-commerce website implemented a chatbot to provide instant support to

customers, resulting in a 15% decrease in the response time and a 10% increase in customer satisfaction.

- How-tos:
    1. Identify Common Queries: Identify the common queries that can be handled by a chatbot. This may involve analyzing the inquiries received by customer service staff or conducting a survey to gather feedback from customers.

    2. Develop the Chatbot: Develop the chatbot to handle the identified common queries. This may involve creating the chatbot script, training the chatbot with sample data, or using a chatbot platform.

    3. Implement the Chatbot: Implement the chatbot on the website or app. This may involve integrating the chatbot with the website or app, testing the chatbot, and making any necessary adjustments.

c. Offer multiple channels of communication: Provide various communication channels such as phone, email, and social media to cater to different customer preferences.

- Explanation: Offering multiple channels of communication can help cater to different customer preferences and increase customer satisfaction.

- Examples:
    1. Phone Support: Offering phone support for customers who prefer to speak to a customer service representative.

    2. Email Support: Offering email support for customers who prefer to communicate via email.

    3. Social Media Support: Offering support via social media channels such as Facebook, Twitter, and Instagram.

- Use Cases:
    1. An online store offered multiple channels of communication, resulting in a 20% increase in customer satisfaction and a 10% increase in repeat purchases.

    2. An e-commerce website offered support via social media channels, resulting in a 15% increase in customer engagement and a 10% increase in customer satisfaction.

- How-tos:
    1. Identify Customer Preferences: Identify the communication channels preferred by the target audience. This may involve conducting a survey or analyzing data on the most commonly used communication channels.

    2. Implement Multiple Channels of Communication: Implement multiple channels of communication on the website or app. This may involve setting up a phone support line, creating an email support address, or setting up social media accounts for customer support.

Case Studies:

1. Amazon: Amazon offers multiple channels of communication, including phone support, email support, and social media support. They also provide regular training to their customer service staff and use chatbots to handle common queries. As a result, Amazon has a high level of customer satisfaction and loyalty.

2. Zappos: Zappos provides regular training to its customer service staff and offers multiple channels of communication, including phone

support, email support, and live chat. They also use chatbots to handle common queries. As a result, Zappos has a high level of customer satisfaction and loyalty.

Overall, improving customer service is crucial for increasing customer satisfaction and loyalty. Providing regular training to customer service staff, implementing chatbots, and offering multiple channels of communication are effective ways to achieve this goal.

Shipping Costs

Objective: Reduce shipping costs to increase competitiveness and profit margins.

Outcome: Lower shipping costs, leading to increased competitiveness and higher profit margins.

Steps: a. Negotiate with shipping providers: Regularly negotiate with shipping providers to get the best rates.

- Explanation: Regularly negotiating with shipping providers can help in getting better rates and reducing overall shipping costs.

- Examples:
    1. Volume Discounts: Negotiating volume-based discounts with shipping providers.

    2. Contract Negotiations: Negotiating long-term contracts with shipping providers for better rates.

- Use Cases:
    1. An online store negotiated a volume-based discount with a shipping provider, resulting in a 20% reduction in shipping costs.

2. An e-commerce website negotiated a long-term contract with a shipping provider, resulting in a 15% reduction in shipping costs.

- How-tos:
    1. Identify Key Shipping Providers: Identify the key shipping providers used by the business. This may involve analyzing the shipping providers used in the past and identifying the ones that offer the best service and rates.

    2. Prepare for Negotiation: Prepare for the negotiation by gathering data on shipping volumes, shipping costs, and the rates offered by competitors.

    3. Negotiate with Shipping Providers: Regularly negotiate with the key shipping providers to get better rates. This may involve negotiating volume-based discounts, long-term contracts, or other favorable terms.

b. Offer free shipping above a certain order value: Encourage customers to purchase more by offering free shipping above a certain order value.

- Explanation: Offering free shipping above a certain order value can encourage customers to purchase more, resulting in higher order values and offsetting the shipping costs.

- Examples:
    1. Free Shipping Threshold: Offering free shipping for orders above $50.

    2. Tiered Shipping Rates: Offering reduced shipping rates for higher order values.

- Use Cases:
    1. An online store offered free shipping for orders above $50, resulting in a 10% increase in the average order value.

    2. An e-commerce website offered tiered shipping rates for higher order values, resulting in a 15% increase in the average order value.

- How-tos:
    1. Analyze Order Values: Analyze the order values to determine the appropriate threshold for free shipping. This may involve analyzing the average order value, the distribution of order values, and the shipping costs.

    2. Determine the Free Shipping Threshold: Determine the appropriate threshold for free shipping. This may involve

calculating the impact on profit margins and competitiveness.

3. Implement the Free Shipping Offer: Implement the free shipping offer on the website or app. This may involve updating the website or app, informing the customers, and monitoring the impact on order values and profit margins.

Case Studies:

1. Amazon: Amazon offers free shipping for orders above a certain value for its Prime members. This has resulted in higher order values and increased loyalty among its Prime members.

2. Zappos: Zappos offers free shipping and free returns for all orders. This has resulted in higher customer satisfaction and loyalty.

Overall, reducing shipping costs is crucial for increasing competitiveness and profit margins. Regularly negotiating with shipping providers and offering free shipping above a certain order value are effective ways to achieve this goal.

Inventory Management

Objective: Improve inventory management to reduce stockouts and carrying costs.

Outcome: Lower rate of stockouts and carrying costs, leading to increased competitiveness and profitability.

Steps:

a. Implement an automated inventory management system: Use an automated system to track inventory levels and reorder stock when necessary.

- Explanation: An automated inventory management system helps in tracking inventory levels in real-time and automatically reorders stock when it reaches a certain level. This reduces the chances of stockouts and carrying costs.

- Examples:
    1. Using an Inventory Management Software: Using software like Zoho Inventory or QuickBooks Commerce that automatically tracks inventory levels and reorders stock when necessary.

    2. Implementing a Just-In-Time (JIT) System: Implementing a JIT system that orders inventory as and when needed.

- Use Cases:
    1. A retail company implemented an automated inventory management system and reduced stockouts by 20% and carrying costs by 15%.

    2. An e-commerce company implemented a JIT system and reduced its carrying costs by 25%.

- How-tos:
    1. Choose the Right Inventory Management System: Choose an inventory management system that fits the needs of the business. This may involve evaluating different systems, considering factors like features, integrations, and pricing.

    2. Implement the Inventory Management System: Implement the chosen inventory management system. This may involve configuring the system, importing existing inventory data, and training staff.

    3. Monitor and Optimize the System: Monitor the performance of the inventory management system and optimize it as necessary. This may involve adjusting reorder points and

quantities, and optimizing the inventory levels.

b. Regularly review inventory levels: Regularly review inventory levels and adjust reorder points and quantities as necessary.

- Explanation: Regularly reviewing inventory levels and adjusting reorder points and quantities helps in maintaining optimal inventory levels and reducing carrying costs.

- Examples:
    1. Monthly Inventory Review: Conducting a monthly review of inventory levels and adjusting reorder points and quantities as necessary.

    2. Seasonal Inventory Adjustment: Adjusting inventory levels and reorder points based on seasonal demand patterns.

- Use Cases:
    1. A fashion retailer conducted a monthly inventory review and adjusted its reorder points and quantities, resulting in a 10% reduction in carrying costs.

    2. An online store adjusted its inventory levels and reorder points based on

seasonal demand patterns, resulting in a 15% reduction in stockouts.

- How-tos:
  1. Analyze Inventory Data: Analyze inventory data to determine the optimal inventory levels and reorder points. This may involve analyzing past sales data, inventory turnover rates, and carrying costs.

  2. Adjust Reorder Points and Quantities: Adjust the reorder points and quantities based on the analysis. This may involve increasing or decreasing the reorder points and quantities for certain products.

  3. Monitor Inventory Levels: Regularly monitor inventory levels and adjust reorder points and quantities as necessary. This may involve conducting regular inventory reviews and adjusting inventory levels based on changing demand patterns.

Case Studies:

1. Toyota: Toyota implemented a JIT system, which helped in reducing carrying costs and

increasing efficiency. This approach has been widely adopted by other companies as well.

2. Zara: Zara uses an advanced inventory management system that helps in maintaining optimal inventory levels and reducing stockouts and carrying costs. This has been a key factor in Zara's success.

Overall, improving inventory management is crucial for reducing stockouts and carrying costs and increasing competitiveness and profitability. Implementing an automated inventory management system and regularly reviewing inventory levels are effective ways to achieve this goal.

Product Descriptions

Objective: Improve product descriptions to increase conversion rates and customer satisfaction.

Outcome: Higher conversion rates and customer satisfaction, leading to increased sales and repeat purchases.

Steps:

a. Provide detailed and accurate product descriptions: Ensure that product descriptions are detailed, accurate, and engaging.

- Explanation: Detailed, accurate, and engaging product descriptions help the customer understand the product better, leading to higher conversion rates and customer satisfaction.

- Examples:
    1. Highlighting Key Features: Highlighting the key features of the product in bullet points.

    2. Storytelling: Using storytelling to describe the product and connect with the customer.

- Use Cases:
    1. An online electronics store provided detailed and accurate product descriptions, resulting in a 15% increase in conversion rates.

    2. A fashion retailer used storytelling in its product descriptions, resulting in a 10% increase in customer satisfaction.

- How-tos:
    1. Analyze Existing Product Descriptions: Analyze the existing product descriptions and identify areas for improvement. This may involve reviewing the product descriptions for accuracy, detail, and engagement.

    2. Create Detailed and Accurate Product Descriptions: Create detailed and accurate product descriptions that highlight the key features of the product and connect with the customer. This may involve writing new product descriptions or improving existing ones.

    3. Test and Optimize Product Descriptions: Test the new product descriptions and optimize them as necessary. This may involve conducting A/B tests to compare different versions of the product

descriptions and analyzing the results to identify the most effective version.

b. Use high-quality images: Use high-quality images that clearly show the product from multiple angles.

- Explanation: High-quality images help the customer visualize the product better, leading to higher conversion rates and customer satisfaction.

- Examples:
    1. Multiple Angles: Showing the product from multiple angles.

    2. Zoom Functionality: Providing a zoom functionality to view the product in detail.

- Use Cases:
    1. An online furniture store used high-quality images that clearly showed the product from multiple angles, resulting in a 20% increase in conversion rates.

    2. An online shoe store provided a zoom functionality to view the shoes in detail, resulting in a 15% increase in customer satisfaction.

- How-tos:
    1. Take High-Quality Images: Take high-quality images of the product from multiple angles. This may involve using a professional camera and lighting equipment.

    2. Edit the Images: Edit the images to ensure they are clear and represent the product accurately. This may involve adjusting the brightness, contrast, and color balance.

    3. Upload the Images: Upload the images to the website or app. This may involve resizing the images, adding alt tags, and testing the images on different devices and screen sizes.

Case Studies:

1. ASOS: ASOS provides detailed and accurate product descriptions and high-quality images that clearly show the product from multiple angles. This has resulted in higher conversion rates and customer satisfaction.

2. Amazon: Amazon provides detailed product descriptions and high-quality images for its products. This has been a key factor in Amazon's success.

Overall, improving product descriptions is crucial for increasing conversion rates and customer satisfaction. Providing detailed and accurate product descriptions and using high-quality images are effective ways to achieve this goal.

Website Navigation

Objective: Improve website navigation to enhance user experience and increase conversion rates.

Outcome: Improved user experience and higher conversion rates, leading to increased sales and customer satisfaction.

Steps:

a. Implement a clear and intuitive site structure: Ensure that the site structure is clear and intuitive, with easy-to-find categories and products.

- Explanation: A clear and intuitive site structure helps the user find the products they are looking for easily, leading to higher conversion rates and customer satisfaction.

- Examples:
    1. Hierarchical Structure: Organizing the categories and products in a hierarchical structure.

    2. Breadcrumb Navigation: Implementing breadcrumb navigation to show the user's path from the homepage to the current page.

- Use Cases:
    1. An online bookstore implemented a clear and intuitive site structure, resulting in a 20% increase in conversion rates.

    2. An online electronics store implemented breadcrumb navigation, resulting in a 15% increase in customer satisfaction.

- How-tos:
    1. Analyze the Existing Site Structure: Analyze the existing site structure and identify areas for improvement. This may involve conducting user research to understand how users navigate the site and identify any pain points.

    2. Create a Clear and Intuitive Site Structure: Create a clear and intuitive site structure that helps the user find the products they are looking for easily. This may involve organizing the categories and products in a hierarchical structure and implementing breadcrumb navigation.

    3. Test and Optimize the Site Structure: Test the new site structure and optimize it as necessary. This may involve conducting usability tests to identify any

issues and optimizing the site structure based on the feedback received.

b. Use clear and descriptive labels: Use clear and descriptive labels for navigation menus and categories.

- Explanation: Clear and descriptive labels help the user understand the contents of each category and navigate the site more easily.

- Examples:
    1. Descriptive Labels: Using descriptive labels like "Women's Shoes" instead of generic labels like "Shoes".

    2. Avoiding Jargon: Avoiding jargon and using language that is familiar to the user.

- Use Cases:
    1. An online fashion store used clear and descriptive labels for its navigation menus and categories, resulting in a 10% increase in conversion rates.

    2. An online sports store avoided jargon and used language that was familiar to the user, resulting in a 5% increase in customer satisfaction.

- How-tos:
  1. Review Existing Labels: Review the existing labels for navigation menus and categories and identify areas for improvement.

  2. Create Clear and Descriptive Labels: Create clear and descriptive labels for navigation menus and categories. This may involve using descriptive labels and avoiding jargon.

  3. Test and Optimize the Labels: Test the new labels and optimize them as necessary. This may involve conducting usability tests to identify any issues and optimizing the labels based on the feedback received.

Case Studies:

1. IKEA: IKEA has a clear and intuitive site structure with clear and descriptive labels for its navigation menus and categories. This has resulted in improved user experience and higher conversion rates.

2. Zalando: Zalando has a clear and intuitive site structure with clear and descriptive labels for its navigation menus and categories. This has been a key factor in Zalando's success.

Overall, improving website navigation is crucial for enhancing user experience and increasing conversion rates. Implementing a clear and intuitive site structure and using clear and descriptive labels for navigation menus and categories are effective ways to achieve this goal.

Payment Security

Objective: Improve payment security to increase customer trust and conversion rates.

Outcome: Higher customer trust and conversion rates, leading to increased sales and customer loyalty.

Steps:

a. Implement SSL certificates: Use SSL certificates to encrypt data transferred between the user's browser and the website.

- Explanation: SSL (Secure Sockets Layer) certificates encrypt the data transferred between the user's browser and the website, ensuring that sensitive information like credit card details and passwords are secure.

- Examples:
    1. Purchasing SSL Certificates: Purchase SSL certificates from a trusted certificate authority (CA) like Verisign or Comodo.

    2. Installing SSL Certificates: Install the SSL certificates on the server hosting the website.

- Use Cases:
    1. An online clothing store implemented SSL certificates and saw a 30% increase in conversion rates as customers felt more secure making payments.

    2. An online electronics store implemented SSL certificates and saw a 25% increase in customer loyalty as customers trusted the website with their payment details.

- How-tos:
    1. Purchase SSL Certificates: Purchase SSL certificates from a trusted certificate authority (CA). There are various types of SSL certificates available, so choose one that suits your needs and budget.

    2. Install SSL Certificates: Install the SSL certificates on the server hosting the website. The process of installing SSL certificates varies depending on the web server being used. Consult the documentation provided by the CA and the web server for detailed instructions.

b. Use secure payment gateways: Use secure and reliable payment gateways to process transactions.

- Explanation: Payment gateways are services that process credit card transactions. Using secure and reliable payment gateways ensures that transactions are processed securely, increasing customer trust and conversion rates.

- Examples:
    1. PayPal: A popular and secure payment gateway used by millions of businesses worldwide.

    2. Stripe: Another popular and secure payment gateway that is easy to integrate with websites and mobile apps.

- Use Cases:
    1. An online bookstore used PayPal as its payment gateway and saw a 20% increase in conversion rates as customers trusted PayPal with their payment details.

    2. An online grocery store used Stripe as its payment gateway and saw a 15% increase in customer loyalty as customers found the payment process to be smooth and secure.

- How-tos:
    1. Choose a Payment Gateway: Choose a secure and reliable payment gateway that suits your needs and budget.

Consider factors like transaction fees, ease of integration, and customer support when making your decision.

2. Integrate the Payment Gateway: Integrate the payment gateway with your website. The process of integrating the payment gateway varies depending on the payment gateway being used and the platform on which your website is built. Consult the documentation provided by the payment gateway and your website platform for detailed instructions.

Case Studies:

1. Amazon: Amazon uses secure payment gateways and SSL certificates to ensure that transactions are processed securely. This has been a key factor in Amazon's success as customers trust Amazon with their payment details.

2. eBay: eBay uses secure payment gateways and SSL certificates to ensure that transactions are processed securely. This has resulted in higher customer trust and conversion rates for eBay.

Overall, improving payment security is crucial for increasing customer trust and conversion rates.

Implementing SSL certificates and using secure payment gateways are effective ways to achieve this goal.

Customer Reviews

Objective: Increase the number of customer reviews to improve social proof and conversion rates.

Outcome: Higher number of customer reviews, leading to increased social proof, higher conversion rates, and increased sales.

Steps:

a. Encourage customer reviews: Actively encourage customers to leave reviews by sending follow-up emails or offering incentives.

- Explanation: Customer reviews are crucial for building social proof and increasing conversion rates. Actively encouraging customers to leave reviews by sending follow-up emails or offering incentives can help increase the number of customer reviews.

- Examples:
    1. Follow-up Emails: Send follow-up emails to customers after they have received their purchase, asking them to leave a review.

    2. Incentives: Offer incentives such as discounts on future purchases or entry

into a prize draw in exchange for leaving a review.

- Use Cases:
    1. An online fashion store sent follow-up emails to customers asking them to leave a review and saw a 40% increase in the number of customer reviews.
    2. An online electronics store offered a 10% discount on future purchases in exchange for leaving a review and saw a 30% increase in the number of customer reviews.

- How-tos:
    1. Set up an Email Campaign: Set up an email campaign to send follow-up emails to customers after they have received their purchase, asking them to leave a review. Use an email marketing tool like Mailchimp or Constant Contact to automate the process.

    2. Offer Incentives: Offer incentives such as discounts on future purchases or entry into a prize draw in exchange for leaving a review. Make sure to clearly communicate the incentive to customers and ensure that it is easy for them to leave a review.

b. Display customer reviews prominently: Display customer reviews prominently on product pages and other relevant areas of the website.

- Explanation: Displaying customer reviews prominently on product pages and other relevant areas of the website helps build social proof and can lead to higher conversion rates.

- Examples:
    1. Product Pages: Display customer reviews prominently on product pages, preferably near the 'Add to Cart' button.
    2. Homepage: Display selected customer reviews on the homepage to immediately build social proof.

- Use Cases:
    1. An online beauty store displayed customer reviews prominently on product pages and saw a 20% increase in conversion rates.

    2. An online sports store displayed selected customer reviews on its homepage and saw a 15% increase in conversion rates.

- How-tos:
    1. Choose the Right Position: Choose the right position on the product pages and

other relevant areas of the website to display customer reviews. The position should be easily visible to visitors without them having to scroll.

2. Use a Review Plugin: Use a review plugin or tool to display customer reviews on your website. Many e-commerce platforms like Shopify and WooCommerce offer review plugins that can be easily integrated into your website.

Case Studies:

1. Amazon: Amazon actively encourages customers to leave reviews by sending follow-up emails and displaying customer reviews prominently on product pages. This has helped Amazon build social proof and increase conversion rates.
2. Zappos: Zappos encourages customers to leave reviews by offering incentives and displaying customer reviews prominently on product pages. This has resulted in a higher number of customer reviews and increased conversion rates for Zappos.

Overall, increasing the number of customer reviews is crucial for building social proof and increasing conversion rates. Actively encouraging customers to leave reviews and displaying them prominently on the website are effective ways to achieve this goal.

Out of Stock Items

Objective: Reduce the rate of out of stock items to improve customer satisfaction and competitiveness.

Outcome: Lower rate of out of stock items, leading to higher customer satisfaction and increased competitiveness.

Steps:

a. Implement an efficient inventory management system: Use an automated inventory management system to track inventory levels and reorder stock when necessary.

- Explanation: An efficient inventory management system can help to track inventory levels in real-time and automatically reorder stock when it falls below a certain level, thereby reducing the rate of out of stock items.

- Examples:
    1. Automated Inventory Management System: Use an automated inventory management system like QuickBooks Commerce or Zoho Inventory to track inventory levels and reorder stock when necessary.

- Use Cases:
    1. An online grocery store implemented an automated inventory management system and reduced the rate of out of stock items by 25%.

    2. An online fashion store implemented an automated inventory management system and saw a 30% decrease in lost sales due to out of stock items.

- How-tos:
    1. Choose the Right System: Choose an inventory management system that fits your business needs and budget. Consider factors like the number of products you sell, the complexity of your supply chain, and the level of automation you need.

    2. Set Reorder Points and Quantities: Set reorder points and quantities for each product in your inventory. The reorder point is the inventory level at which a new order should be placed, and the reorder quantity is the amount of the product that should be ordered.

b. Regularly review inventory levels: Regularly review inventory levels and adjust reorder points and quantities as necessary.

- Explanation: Regularly reviewing inventory levels and adjusting reorder points and quantities as necessary can help to ensure that you always have the right amount of stock on hand and reduce the rate of out of stock items.

- Examples:
    1. Monthly Inventory Review: Conduct a monthly review of inventory levels and adjust reorder points and quantities as necessary.

- Use Cases:
    1. An online electronics store conducted a monthly review of inventory levels and adjusted reorder points and quantities as necessary, resulting in a 20% reduction in the rate of out of stock items.

    2. An online beauty store regularly reviewed inventory levels and adjusted reorder points and quantities as necessary, leading to a 15% increase in customer satisfaction due to the availability of products.

- How-tos:
    1. Set a Schedule: Set a schedule for reviewing inventory levels. This could be weekly, monthly, or quarterly,

depending on the nature of your business and the products you sell.

2. Adjust Reorder Points and Quantities: Based on your review, adjust reorder points and quantities as necessary to ensure that you always have the right amount of stock on hand.

Case Studies:

1. Walmart: Walmart uses an automated inventory management system to track inventory levels and reorder stock when necessary. This has helped Walmart to reduce the rate of out of stock items and improve customer satisfaction.

2. Amazon: Amazon regularly reviews inventory levels and adjusts reorder points and quantities as necessary. This has helped Amazon to reduce the rate of out of stock items and improve its competitiveness.

Overall, reducing the rate of out of stock items is crucial for improving customer satisfaction and competitiveness. Implementing an efficient inventory management system and regularly reviewing inventory levels are effective ways to achieve this goal.

Order Processing

Objective: Improve order processing efficiency to reduce order processing times and increase customer satisfaction.

Outcome: Reduced order processing times, leading to higher customer satisfaction and increased competitiveness.

Steps:

a. Implement an automated order processing system: Use an automated system to process orders quickly and accurately.

- Explanation: An automated order processing system can help to process orders quickly and accurately by eliminating manual data entry and minimizing human errors.

- Examples:
    1. Order Management System: Use an order management system like Brightpearl or Orderhive to process orders quickly and accurately.

- Use Cases:
    1. An online book store implemented an automated order processing system and reduced order processing times by 40%.

2. An online food delivery service implemented an automated order processing system and saw a 30% increase in customer satisfaction due to faster order processing times.

- How-tos:
    1. Choose the Right System: Choose an order processing system that fits your business needs and budget. Consider factors like the number of orders you process, the complexity of your order processing workflow, and the level of automation you need.

    2. Set Up the System: Set up the order processing system according to your business requirements. Configure order processing workflows, payment processing, and shipping options.

b. Train staff: Provide regular training to staff involved in order processing to ensure they have the necessary knowledge and skills.

- Explanation: Regular training can help to ensure that staff involved in order processing have the necessary knowledge and skills to use the automated system efficiently and process orders accurately.

- Examples:
    1. Online Training Modules: Develop online training modules that staff can complete at their own pace.

    2. Regular Training Sessions: Conduct regular training sessions to provide staff with the latest updates and best practices.

- Use Cases:
    1. An online electronics store provided regular training to its order processing staff and saw a 20% reduction in order processing errors.

    2. An online fashion store provided regular training to its order processing staff and saw a 15% increase in order processing efficiency.

- How-tos:
    1. Develop a Training Program: Develop a training program that covers all aspects of order processing, including using the automated system, handling special order types, and dealing with common issues.

    2. Conduct Regular Training: Conduct regular training sessions to provide staff

with the latest updates and best practices. This could be monthly or quarterly, depending on the nature of your business and the complexity of your order processing workflow.

Case Studies:

1. Zappos: Zappos uses an automated order processing system to process orders quickly and accurately. It also provides regular training to its order processing staff to ensure they have the necessary knowledge and skills. This has helped Zappos to reduce order processing times and increase customer satisfaction.

2. Shopify: Shopify provides an automated order processing system to its merchants and offers online training modules and regular training sessions to help them use the system efficiently and process orders accurately. This has helped Shopify merchants to reduce order processing times and increase customer satisfaction.

Overall, improving order processing efficiency is crucial for reducing order processing times and increasing customer satisfaction. Implementing an automated order processing system and providing regular training to staff involved in order processing are effective ways to achieve this goal.

Order Fulfillment

Objective: Improve order fulfillment efficiency to reduce order fulfillment times and increase customer satisfaction.

Outcome: Reduced order fulfillment times, leading to higher customer satisfaction and increased competitiveness.

Steps:

a. Optimize the supply chain: Regularly review and optimize the supply chain to ensure it is as efficient as possible.

- Explanation: Optimizing the supply chain involves reviewing and improving all processes related to sourcing, manufacturing, transportation, and delivery of products. This can help to reduce order fulfillment times and increase customer satisfaction.

- Examples:
    1. Supplier Relationship Management: Develop strong relationships with suppliers to ensure a steady supply of materials and products.

    2. Just-in-Time Inventory: Implement just-in-time inventory practices to reduce

carrying costs and improve inventory turnover.

- Use Cases:
  1. An online electronics store optimized its supply chain by developing strong relationships with suppliers and implementing just-in-time inventory practices. This helped to reduce order fulfillment times by 30%.

  2. An online fashion store optimized its supply chain by consolidating shipments and negotiating better shipping rates. This helped to reduce shipping costs by 20%.

- How-tos:
  1. Conduct a Supply Chain Audit: Conduct a comprehensive audit of your supply chain to identify areas for improvement. This includes reviewing supplier relationships, inventory practices, transportation options, and delivery processes.

  2. Develop an Optimization Plan: Develop a plan to optimize your supply chain. This may involve developing stronger relationships with suppliers, implementing just-in-time inventory

practices, consolidating shipments, and negotiating better shipping rates.

b. Implement automated fulfillment processes: Use automated processes to pick, pack, and ship orders quickly and accurately.

- Explanation: Automated fulfillment processes can help to reduce manual labor, minimize errors, and speed up the order fulfillment process.

- Examples:
    1. Automated Picking System: Implement an automated picking system to quickly and accurately pick items from the warehouse.

    2. Automated Packing System: Implement an automated packing system to pack orders quickly and accurately.

- Use Cases:
    1. An online book store implemented automated picking and packing systems and saw a 40% reduction in order fulfillment times.

    2. An online food delivery service implemented automated packing and

shipping systems and saw a 25% reduction in order fulfillment errors.

- How-tos:
    1. Evaluate Your Needs: Evaluate your order fulfillment needs and determine the level of automation required. This will depend on the volume of orders, the complexity of the order fulfillment process, and your budget.

    2. Choose the Right Technology: Choose the right technology for your automated fulfillment processes. This may involve implementing an automated picking system, an automated packing system, or both.

Case Studies:

1. Amazon: Amazon has optimized its supply chain and implemented automated fulfillment processes to reduce order fulfillment times and increase customer satisfaction. This includes using robots to pick and pack items in its fulfillment centers and using drones for delivery in certain areas.

2. Zalando: Zalando has optimized its supply chain by developing strong relationships with suppliers and implementing just-in-time

inventory practices. It has also implemented automated fulfillment processes, including automated picking and packing systems, to reduce order fulfillment times and increase customer satisfaction.

Overall, improving order fulfillment efficiency is crucial for reducing order fulfillment times and increasing customer satisfaction. Optimizing the supply chain and implementing automated fulfillment processes are effective ways to achieve this goal.

Marketing Strategy

Objective: Develop and implement an effective marketing strategy to increase brand awareness, traffic, and conversions.

Outcome: Increased brand awareness, website traffic, and conversion rates, leading to higher sales and customer loyalty.

Steps:

a. Develop a comprehensive marketing strategy: Develop a strategy that includes SEO, PPC, email marketing, and social media marketing.

- Explanation: A comprehensive marketing strategy includes various digital marketing tactics such as SEO, PPC, email marketing, and social media marketing. This ensures that you are reaching your target audience through multiple channels and maximizing your chances of success.

- Examples:
    1. SEO: Optimizing your website for search engines to increase its visibility in organic search results.

2. PPC: Running paid ads on search engines and social media platforms to drive traffic and conversions.

3. Email Marketing: Sending targeted emails to your subscribers to encourage them to visit your website and make a purchase.

4. Social Media Marketing: Using social media platforms to promote your brand, products, and content.

- Use Cases:
    1. A fashion retailer developed a comprehensive marketing strategy that included SEO, PPC, email marketing, and social media marketing. This helped to increase its brand awareness, website traffic, and conversion rates by 30%.

    2. An electronics retailer developed a comprehensive marketing strategy that included SEO, PPC, email marketing, and social media marketing. This helped to increase its brand awareness, website traffic, and conversion rates by 40%.

- How-tos:
    1. Conduct a Marketing Audit: Conduct a comprehensive audit of your current

marketing efforts to identify strengths, weaknesses, opportunities, and threats.

2. Set Marketing Goals: Set clear and measurable marketing goals based on your business objectives.

3. Develop a Marketing Plan: Develop a comprehensive marketing plan that includes strategies and tactics for SEO, PPC, email marketing, and social media marketing.

b. Regularly monitor and adjust the strategy: Regularly monitor the performance of the marketing strategy and adjust it as necessary.

- Explanation: Regularly monitoring the performance of your marketing strategy allows you to identify what is working and what is not, and make necessary adjustments to optimize its effectiveness.

- Examples:
    1. Using Google Analytics to monitor website traffic, user behavior, and conversion rates.

    2. Using an email marketing platform to monitor email open rates, click-through rates, and conversion rates.

- Use Cases:
  1. A fashion retailer regularly monitored the performance of its marketing strategy using Google Analytics and an email marketing platform. This helped to identify underperforming tactics and make necessary adjustments, leading to a 20% increase in conversion rates.

  2. An electronics retailer regularly monitored the performance of its marketing strategy using Google Analytics and an email marketing platform. This helped to identify underperforming tactics and make necessary adjustments, leading to a 25% increase in conversion rates.

- How-tos:
  1. Implement Monitoring Tools: Implement tools such as Google Analytics, Google Ads, and an email marketing platform to monitor the performance of your marketing strategy.

  2. Establish a Monitoring Schedule: Establish a schedule for regularly monitoring the performance of your marketing strategy. This may involve reviewing key performance indicators (KPIs) daily, weekly, or monthly.

Case Studies:

1. Amazon: Amazon is a global online retailer that has developed a comprehensive marketing strategy that includes SEO, PPC, email marketing, and social media marketing. Amazon regularly monitors the performance of its marketing strategy and adjusts it as necessary. This has helped to increase its brand awareness, website traffic, and conversion rates, leading to higher sales and customer loyalty.

2. Apple: Apple is a global technology company that has developed a comprehensive marketing strategy that includes SEO, PPC, email marketing, and social media marketing. Apple regularly monitors the performance of its marketing strategy and adjusts it as necessary. This has helped to increase its brand awareness, website traffic, and conversion rates, leading to higher sales and customer loyalty.

Overall, developing and implementing an effective marketing strategy is crucial for increasing brand awareness, website traffic, and conversions. Developing a comprehensive marketing strategy and regularly monitoring and adjusting it are effective ways to achieve this goal.

Product Images

Objective: Use high-quality product images to increase conversion rates and customer satisfaction.

Outcome: Higher conversion rates and customer satisfaction, leading to increased sales and repeat purchases.

Steps:

a. Use high-quality images: Use high-resolution images that clearly show the product from multiple angles.

- Explanation: High-quality images are crucial for online retail as they are the only way customers can 'see' the product before purchasing. High-resolution images that clearly show the product from multiple angles give customers a better sense of what they are buying, increasing their confidence in their purchase decision.

- Examples:
    1. A fashion retailer uses high-resolution images that clearly show the clothing items from multiple angles, including front, back, and side views.

    2. An electronics retailer uses high-resolution images that clearly show the

product from multiple angles, including top, bottom, front, and back views.

- Use Cases:
    1. A fashion retailer found that by using high-resolution images that clearly show the clothing items from multiple angles, it was able to increase its conversion rates by 20%.

    2. An electronics retailer found that by using high-resolution images that clearly show the product from multiple angles, it was able to increase its conversion rates by 25%.

- How-tos:
    1. Hire a Professional Photographer: If possible, hire a professional photographer to take high-quality images of your products.

    2. Use a High-Quality Camera: If hiring a professional photographer is not possible, use a high-quality camera to take images of your products.

    3. Use Proper Lighting: Ensure that the lighting is adequate when taking images of your products. This will ensure that

the images are clear and the colors are accurate.

b. Offer multiple views of the product: Provide multiple views of the product to give customers a better sense of what they are buying.

- Explanation: Providing multiple views of the product allows customers to see the product from different angles, giving them a better sense of what they are buying. This can help to increase their confidence in their purchase decision and reduce the rate of product returns.

- Examples:
    1. A fashion retailer provides multiple views of the clothing items, including front, back, and side views.

    2. An electronics retailer provides multiple views of the product, including top, bottom, front, and back views.

- Use Cases:
    1. A fashion retailer found that by providing multiple views of the clothing items, it was able to reduce its rate of product returns by 15%.

2. An electronics retailer found that by providing multiple views of the product, it was able to reduce its rate of product returns by 20%.

- How-tos:
    1. Use a Turntable: Use a turntable to take images of the product from multiple angles.

    2. Use a Photo Editing Software: Use a photo editing software to edit the images and ensure that they are clear and of high quality.

Case Studies:

1. Zara: Zara is a global fashion retailer that uses high-quality images to increase its conversion rates and customer satisfaction. Zara uses high-resolution images that clearly show the clothing items from multiple angles, including front, back, and side views. This has helped to increase its conversion rates and customer satisfaction, leading to increased sales and repeat purchases.

2. Apple: Apple is a global technology company that uses high-quality images to increase its conversion rates and customer satisfaction. Apple uses high-resolution images that clearly

show the product from multiple angles, including top, bottom, front, and back views. This has helped to increase its conversion rates and customer satisfaction, leading to increased sales and repeat purchases.

Overall, using high-quality product images is crucial for increasing conversion rates and customer satisfaction. Using high-resolution images that clearly show the product from multiple angles and providing multiple views of the product can help to achieve this goal.

Order Tracking

Objective: Implement an order tracking system to increase customer satisfaction and trust.

Outcome: Higher customer satisfaction and trust, leading to increased customer loyalty and repeat purchases.

Steps:

a. Implement an order tracking system: Use a system that allows customers to track their orders in real-time.

- Explanation: An order tracking system allows customers to know where their order is at any given moment, from the time it is placed until it is delivered. This increases customer satisfaction as it reduces anxiety and uncertainty about the status of their order.

- Examples:
    1. Amazon uses an order tracking system that allows customers to track their orders in real-time.

    2. FedEx uses a tracking system that allows customers to track their packages in real-time.

- Use Cases:
    1. An online retailer found that by implementing an order tracking system, it was able to increase its customer satisfaction ratings by 30%.

    2. A shipping company found that by implementing a tracking system, it was able to reduce the number of customer inquiries about the status of their packages by 50%.

- How-tos:
    1. Choose a Tracking System: There are various tracking systems available, both paid and free. Choose one that fits your needs and budget.

    2. Integrate the Tracking System: Integrate the tracking system into your order processing system so that it can provide real-time updates to your customers.

b. Provide regular updates to customers: Send regular updates to customers about the status of their order.

- Explanation: Regular updates about the status of their order, such as when it is processed, shipped, and out for delivery, can help to reduce customer anxiety and increase satisfaction.

- Examples:
    1. Amazon sends regular updates to customers about the status of their order via email and mobile notifications.

    2. FedEx sends regular updates to customers about the status of their package via email and mobile notifications.

- Use Cases:
    1. An online retailer found that by sending regular updates to customers about the status of their order, it was able to reduce the number of customer inquiries about the status of their order by 40%.

    2. A shipping company found that by sending regular updates to customers about the status of their package, it was able to increase its customer satisfaction ratings by 20%.

- How-tos:
    1. Choose a Communication Channel: Determine how you will send updates to your customers. This could be via email, mobile notifications, or both.

2. Automate the Updates: Use an automated system to send updates to your customers at each stage of the order process.

Case Studies:

1. Amazon: Amazon is a global online retailer that uses an order tracking system to increase customer satisfaction and trust. Amazon uses a system that allows customers to track their orders in real-time and sends regular updates to customers about the status of their order via email and mobile notifications. This has helped to increase customer satisfaction and trust, leading to increased customer loyalty and repeat purchases.

2. FedEx: FedEx is a global shipping company that uses a tracking system to increase customer satisfaction and trust. FedEx uses a system that allows customers to track their packages in real-time and sends regular updates to customers about the status of their package via email and mobile notifications. This has helped to increase customer satisfaction and trust, leading to increased customer loyalty and repeat purchases.

Overall, implementing an order tracking system and providing regular updates to customers about the status of their order can help to increase customer satisfaction and trust, leading to increased customer loyalty and repeat purchases.

Customer Loyalty

Objective: Implement a customer loyalty program to increase customer retention and repeat purchases.

Outcome: Higher customer retention and repeat purchases, leading to increased sales and profitability.

Steps:

a. Implement a customer loyalty program: Develop and implement a program that rewards customers for repeat purchases.

- Explanation: A customer loyalty program rewards customers for their repeat business. It typically involves giving customers points for every purchase, which can then be redeemed for discounts, gifts, or other rewards. This encourages customers to keep coming back and making purchases from your business.

- Examples:
    1. Starbucks Rewards: A loyalty program where customers earn stars for every purchase, which can be redeemed for free drinks, food, or merchandise.

    2. Sephora Beauty Insider: A loyalty program where customers earn points for every purchase, which can be

redeemed for discounts, gifts, or special offers.

- Use Cases:
    1. A retailer found that by implementing a customer loyalty program, it was able to increase its customer retention rate by 20%.

    2. A restaurant found that by implementing a customer loyalty program, it was able to increase its repeat business by 30%.

- How-tos:
    1. Choose a Program Type: Decide what type of loyalty program you want to implement. This could be a points-based program, a tiered program, or another type of program.

    2. Determine the Rewards: Decide what rewards you will offer to your customers. This could be discounts, gifts, special offers, or other rewards.

    3. Implement the Program: Use a software solution or app to implement the program and keep track of customers' purchases and rewards.

b. Regularly communicate with customers: Send regular updates to customers about new products, promotions, and loyalty program rewards.

- Explanation: Regular communication with customers keeps them engaged and informed about your business. This can help to encourage repeat purchases and increase customer loyalty.

- Examples:
    1. Sephora sends regular emails to its Beauty Insider members with updates on new products, promotions, and loyalty program rewards.

    2. Starbucks sends regular emails and mobile notifications to its Rewards members with updates on new products, promotions, and loyalty program rewards.

- Use Cases:
    1. A retailer found that by sending regular updates to its customers, it was able to increase its email open rate by 25%.

    2. A restaurant found that by sending regular updates to its customers, it was able to increase its repeat business by 15%.

- How-tos:
    1. Choose a Communication Channel: Determine how you will communicate with your customers. This could be via email, mobile notifications, or social media.

    2. Determine the Frequency: Decide how often you will communicate with your customers. This could be daily, weekly, or monthly.

Case Studies:

1. Starbucks: Starbucks is a global coffee company that has implemented a successful customer loyalty program called Starbucks Rewards. This program rewards customers with stars for every purchase, which can be redeemed for free drinks, food, or merchandise. Starbucks also sends regular updates to its Rewards members via email and mobile notifications with updates on new products, promotions, and loyalty program rewards. This has helped to increase customer retention and repeat purchases, leading to increased sales and profitability.

2. Sephora: Sephora is a global beauty retailer that has implemented a successful customer

loyalty program called Sephora Beauty Insider. This program rewards customers with points for every purchase, which can be redeemed for discounts, gifts, or special offers. Sephora also sends regular emails to its Beauty Insider members with updates on new products, promotions, and loyalty program rewards. This has helped to increase customer retention and repeat purchases, leading to increased sales and profitability.

Overall, implementing a customer loyalty program and regularly communicating with customers about new products, promotions, and loyalty program rewards can help to increase customer retention and repeat purchases, leading to increased sales and profitability.

Product Availability

Objective: Ensure product availability to meet customer demand and minimize stockouts.

Outcome: Higher customer satisfaction and sales due to reduced stockouts and better inventory management.

Steps:

a. Implement an advanced inventory management system: Use a system that predicts demand and helps in maintaining optimal inventory levels.

- Explanation: An advanced inventory management system not only tracks inventory levels but also uses algorithms to predict future demand based on historical data, seasonality, and other factors. This helps in maintaining optimal inventory levels, reducing the chances of stockouts or overstocking.

- Examples:
    1. Just-in-time (JIT) inventory system: A system that aims to have inventory arrive just as it is needed, reducing carrying costs.

2. Vendor-managed inventory (VMI): A system where the supplier manages the inventory levels and replenishes stock as needed.

- Use Cases:
    1. A retailer implemented a JIT inventory system and was able to reduce its carrying costs by 20%.

    2. A manufacturer implemented a VMI system with its suppliers and was able to reduce stockouts by 30%.

- How-tos:
    1. Choose the Right System: Determine which inventory management system is best suited for your business needs.

    2. Implement the System: Work with a vendor or an expert to implement the system and train your staff on how to use it.

b. Regularly monitor inventory levels: Keep a close eye on inventory levels and reorder stock well in advance to avoid stockouts.

- Explanation: Regularly monitoring inventory levels helps in identifying fast-moving products and ensures that reorder points and quantities are adjusted as necessary to avoid stockouts.

- Examples:
    1. Using an inventory management software that sends alerts when stock levels fall below a certain point.

    2. Conducting regular physical inventory counts.

- Use Cases:
    1. A retailer used inventory management software to monitor inventory levels and was able to reduce stockouts by 25%.

    2. A wholesaler conducted regular physical inventory counts and was able to identify discrepancies and adjust reorder points accordingly.

- How-tos:
    1. Set Reorder Points and Quantities: Determine the reorder points and quantities for each product based on historical data and future predictions.

    2. Monitor Inventory Levels: Use software or conduct physical counts to regularly monitor inventory levels.

Case Studies:

1. Toyota: Toyota is a global automobile manufacturer that implemented a JIT inventory system, which aims to have inventory arrive just as it is needed. This reduced carrying costs and increased efficiency in its production process. Toyota also works closely with its suppliers and regularly monitors inventory levels to avoid stockouts and ensure product availability.

2. Walmart: Walmart is a global retailer that implemented a VMI system with its suppliers. This means that the suppliers manage the inventory levels and replenish stock as needed. Walmart also uses an advanced inventory management system that predicts demand and helps in maintaining optimal inventory levels. This has helped Walmart in reducing stockouts, increasing customer satisfaction, and improving sales.

Overall, implementing an advanced inventory management system and regularly monitoring inventory levels can help in ensuring product availability, reducing stockouts, and increasing customer satisfaction and sales.

Competitive Pricing

Objective: Implement a competitive pricing strategy to attract and retain customers.

Outcome: Increased sales and customer loyalty due to attractive and competitive pricing.

Steps:

a. Conduct market research: Regularly analyze competitor prices and customer expectations.

- Explanation: Conducting market research involves collecting and analyzing data about the prices of competitor products and the price expectations of customers. This helps in understanding the market trends, identifying the optimal price range for your products, and ensuring that your prices are competitive.

- Examples:
    1. Conducting surveys to understand customer price expectations.

    2. Using online tools to monitor competitor prices.

- Use Cases:
    1. A company conducted a survey and found that customers were willing to

pay more for environmentally friendly products. This helped the company in setting a competitive price for its eco-friendly products.

2. An online retailer used a price monitoring tool to track competitor prices and was able to adjust its prices accordingly to stay competitive.

- How-tos:
    1. Choose the Right Tools: Use online tools, surveys, or hire a market research firm to collect data on competitor prices and customer expectations.

    2. Analyze the Data: Analyze the collected data to identify trends, optimal price ranges, and areas for improvement.

b. Implement a dynamic pricing strategy: Adjust prices in real-time based on market demand, competitor prices, and other factors.

- Explanation: Dynamic pricing involves adjusting prices in real-time based on various factors such as market demand, competitor prices, inventory levels, and seasonality. This helps in maximizing profits, staying competitive, and meeting customer expectations.

- Examples:
    1. Airlines adjust ticket prices in real-time based on demand, seat availability, and competitor prices.

    2. Uber adjusts ride prices in real-time based on demand and supply.

- Use Cases:
    1. A hotel implemented a dynamic pricing strategy and was able to increase its revenue by 15% during the peak season.

    2. An online retailer implemented dynamic pricing and was able to maximize its profits by adjusting prices in real-time based on demand and competitor prices.

- How-tos:
    1. Choose a Dynamic Pricing Tool: Use a dynamic pricing tool or develop a custom solution that allows you to adjust prices in real-time based on various factors.

    2. Set Pricing Rules: Define the rules and factors that will influence your pricing adjustments. For example, increase prices by 10% if demand increases by 20%.

Case Studies:

1. Amazon: Amazon uses dynamic pricing and changes its prices millions of times a day based on various factors such as competitor prices, demand, and inventory levels. This helps Amazon in staying competitive, maximizing profits, and meeting customer expectations.

2. Uber: Uber uses dynamic pricing to adjust ride prices in real-time based on demand and supply. During times of high demand and low supply, prices increase, and during times of low demand and high supply, prices decrease. This helps Uber in balancing demand and supply and maximizing profits.

Overall, implementing a competitive pricing strategy involves conducting market research to understand competitor prices and customer expectations, and implementing a dynamic pricing strategy to adjust prices in real-time based on various factors. This helps in attracting and retaining customers, staying competitive, and maximizing profits.

Payment Options

Objective: Offer multiple payment options to cater to different customer preferences and increase conversion rates.

Outcome: Higher conversion rates and customer satisfaction due to the availability of various payment options.

Steps:

a. Partner with multiple payment providers: Establish partnerships with various payment providers to offer multiple payment options.

- Explanation: Partnering with multiple payment providers allows you to offer a variety of payment options to your customers, catering to their different preferences and increasing the chances of successful transactions.

- Examples:
    1. Partnering with PayPal to offer PayPal as a payment option.
    2. Partnering with Stripe to offer credit card payments.

- Use Cases:
    1. An online store partnered with multiple payment providers and saw a 20%

increase in conversion rates as customers were able to choose their preferred payment method.

2. A subscription service partnered with various payment providers to cater to its international customer base, resulting in increased customer satisfaction and a decrease in payment-related customer service inquiries.

- How-tos:
    1. Research Payment Providers: Research various payment providers and identify the ones that are most popular among your target audience and offer the best terms and conditions.

    2. Establish Partnerships: Contact the selected payment providers and establish partnerships with them.

b. Clearly communicate available payment options: Make sure customers are aware of all available payment options during the checkout process.

- Explanation: Clearly communicating the available payment options during the checkout process ensures that customers are aware of all the options and can choose the one that is most convenient for them.

- Examples:
    1. Listing all available payment options on the checkout page.

    2. Displaying the logos of all available payment options during the checkout process.

- Use Cases:
    1. An online store clearly communicated the available payment options during the checkout process, resulting in a decrease in cart abandonment rates as customers were able to choose their preferred payment method.

    2. A hotel clearly communicated the available payment options during the booking process, resulting in increased customer satisfaction as international customers were able to choose a payment option that was available in their country.

- How-tos:
    1. Update Checkout Page: Update the checkout page to include a list of all available payment options and their logos.

2. Inform Customers: Inform customers about the available payment options through your website, email communications, and marketing materials.

Case Studies:

1. Amazon: Amazon offers multiple payment options, including credit cards, debit cards, Amazon gift cards, and PayPal. This allows Amazon to cater to a wide range of customer preferences and increases the chances of successful transactions.

2. Airbnb: Airbnb offers various payment options, including credit cards, debit cards, PayPal, and Apple Pay. This allows Airbnb to cater to its international customer base and increases customer satisfaction.

Overall, offering multiple payment options involves establishing partnerships with various payment providers and clearly communicating the available payment options during the checkout process. This caters to different customer preferences, increases conversion rates, and enhances customer satisfaction.

Outro

As we draw the curtains on this enlightening journey through the world of e-commerce, I hope you've found the insights and strategies shared to be invaluable. The digital marketplace is a dynamic and ever-evolving entity, and staying ahead requires not just knowledge, but the ability to apply that knowledge effectively. This book was designed to be your compass in this vast ocean, guiding you towards success and profitability.

But remember, the real journey begins now. The pages you've just traversed are filled with actionable steps and strategies, waiting to be implemented. The true potential of this book lies not in its reading, but in its application. Take the lessons learned, apply them to your business, and watch as the magic unfolds.

However, success in e-commerce, as in life, is not just about individual milestones but continuous growth. Stay curious, keep learning, and always be open to adapting and evolving. The digital landscape changes rapidly, and the most successful players are those who change with it.

Lastly, a reminder from Mike Austman himself: your feedback is the beacon that can guide future editions of this book and help others in their e-commerce journey. Whether you've found success using these strategies or faced challenges, your experiences are invaluable. Share them on Twitter @MikeAustman, and be a part of the larger conversation.

Thank you for embarking on this journey with us. Here's to your e-commerce success and to the countless milestones you're destined to achieve!

Best wishes, The Team Behind 23 Potentially Massive Issues E-commerce Businesses Have & How To Fix & Prevent Them